HAPPINESS IS...

1001 tiny moments of happiness

©2024 Lisa Swerling & Ralph Lazar
www.lastlemon.com

Book design by Lisa Swerling & Ralph Lazar
Published by Last Lemon Productions
London N19 United Kingdom

ISBN 9798332528576

First printing 2024

HAPPINESS IS...

1001 tiny moments of happiness

a card from someone
far away

butter melting into
hot toast

waking up to snow

reaching the top

the golden glow of a jar
of honey in sunlight

rearranging the
contents of the fridge
to get more space

the random sniffiness
of dogs

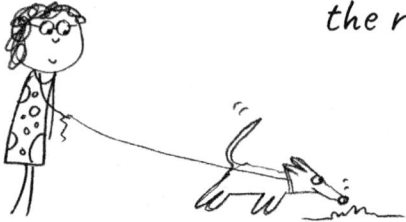

a cat lying on
your knees

solitude

finding the lost remote

flying a kite

pure alone time
when traveling

when the doctor tells you
it's the last surgery

celebrating
your favorite
team's win

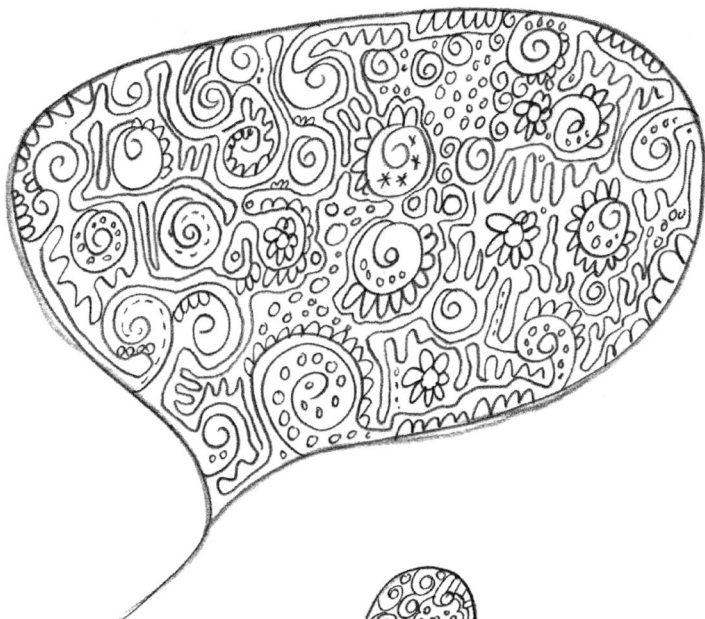

feeling understood

drying off
in the hot sun

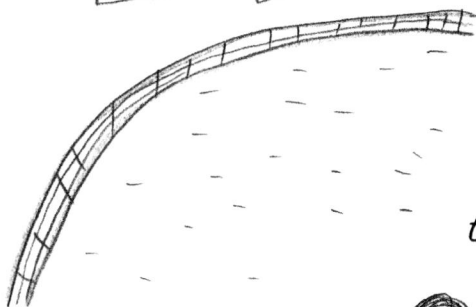

tickle wars

pure fruit juice

the nice smell of someone you like still on their clothes

a 'ta-da' moment

starting a new book

playing a great tune
on an old guitar

sneaking a late night
bowl of cereal

an unexpected credit
in your bank account

rowing

a really good
potato peeler

wearing pajamas all day

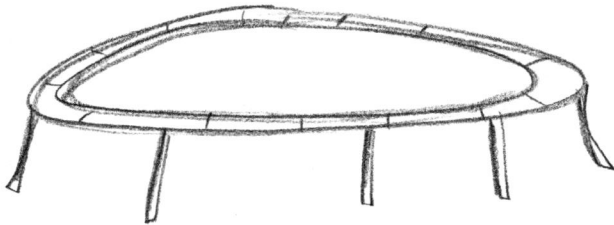

jumping as high as you can

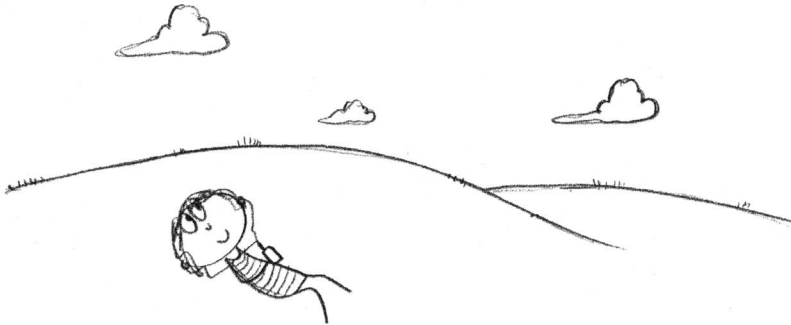

watching clouds float by

winning a trophy

a pizza all to yourself

being asked if you
want to join in

messy art

dancing along
to a show

a relaxed holiday

singing together

making new friends
through music

sucking honey
from a spoon

studying hard
and hoping for
the best

a clean desktop

going fast

an unexpected
day off

going
backpacking

mom beside
you

a glass wall

playing in the waves

wiping dirty hands
on your apron

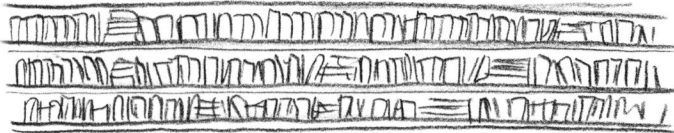

a secret crush

being there for someone who's
always been there for you

finding someone with the
same taste as you

hugs

being friends
with an ex

dog walks

a hot shower
on a cold day

family games

a new sofa

snapping a tape
measure back in

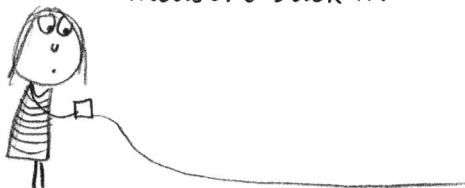

making a friend
laugh

an unputdownable
book

winning an online
auction

friends who are a little bit
different

a deep catch-up

cycling on a
summer morning

pulling secret faces
at a child

big treats for small
creatures

children laughing about how
people lived in the old days

untangling a chain necklace
that has a knot

jogging in a city you love
listening to music you love

activities with friends

feeling your teeth
with your tongue
after brushing them

life-long learning

finishing admin
on time

planning for the
weekend on Monday

hand-holding

cuddling after a day
running around

an inspirational
conversation

remaining hopeful while
accepting hardship

phew!

recovering deleted
files

regular exercise

the first picnic of spring

a beach bungalow hidden in the trees

falling asleep
to purrs

waking up thinking it's Monday, but it's actually Sunday

finding the biggest potato chip in the packet

a day at home just chilling

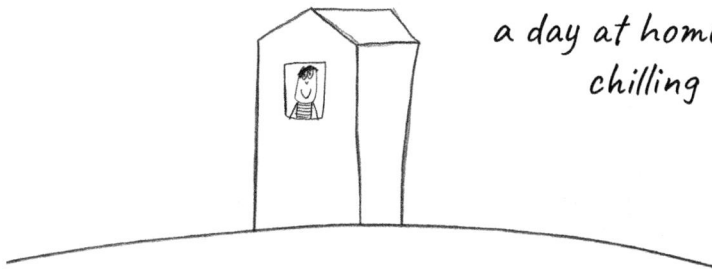

meditating

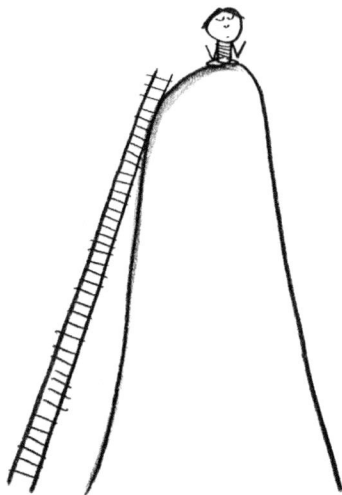

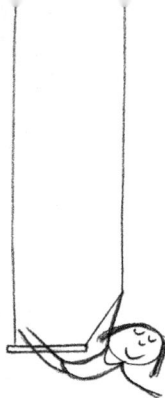

being nimble

laying out all your
new clothes

making a friend
happy

specks of dust
in sunlight

the sound of a little object being sucked upwards
through the vacuum cleaner

licking ice-cream drips

the last petal ending
on 'loves me'

looking good with
short hair

day-dreaming

control of the remote

returning home

thinking exactly
the same thing at
exactly the same moment

CAFÉ

watching the world go by

when you've still 'got it'

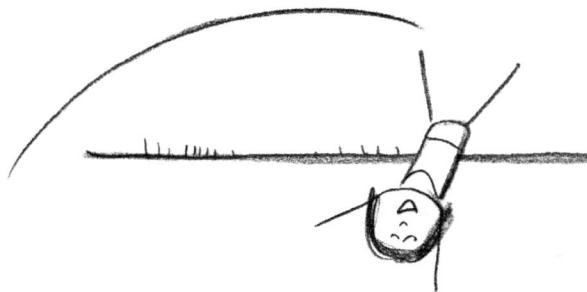

a new tool for
the man cave

a stranger smiling back

a loving toast

corn-on-the-cob

a double-treat from a
malfunctioning vending
machine

writing poetry

carving the roast

the first cup of coffee
after you have given up
giving it up

colorful sticky
notes

drinking out of small
teacups

time in the park

gently covering a
seed you've put in
the ground

when your favorite
song comes on

a long bath

when your parents
appreciate the way
you've chosen to live
your life

laughing out
loud at a funny
thought

making travel plans

feeling far from everything

wrapping neatly

the belief in true love
even after heartbreak

diving into a
pool, into the
underwater
silence

a tiny ladybug

candlelight

yawning freely when
you're alone

waking up to sunshine

handmade
knitwear

a midday nap

lots of birthday candles

going through old diaries

eating with chopsticks

flying through clouds

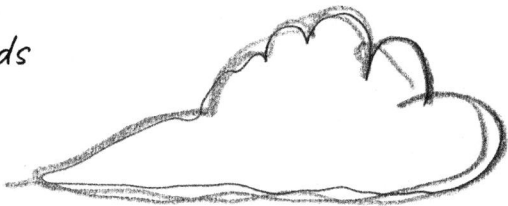

RING!

the moment the pizza guy rings the door bell

having a marker pen handy just when you need it

a perfectly tossed salad

inter-generational gossip

giving away the bigger piece of chocolate

when your friends are impressed
by your mom's cooking
and you're so proud of her

wearing the first summer
dress of the season

annoying your elder sister
by being taller than her

a cup of warm milk
with honey and cinnamon

not having to wake up early

realizing your hiccups
have stopped

starting to
plan a holiday

one fluffy white cloud
in a blue sky

childhood
friend groups

when your online order
looks even better than
you'd hoped

radiating good vibes

being a pro at work

a BBQ in winter

building a
blanket fort

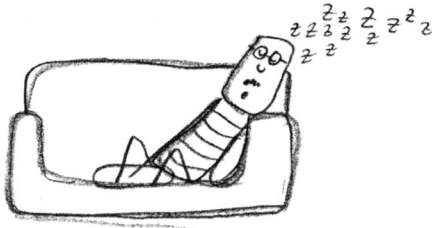

grandpa snores from
the couch

wiggling your toes
outside the blanket
for the cat to catch

karaoke when you're
home alone

the sound of a child's laughter

picking cherries

realizing you are
actually a good
cook

waking up really early,
peeing, then going back to bed

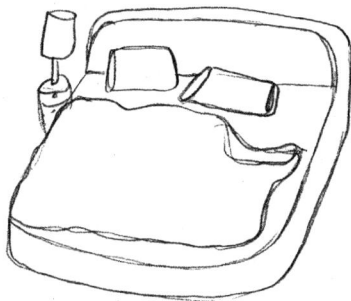

learning a
new skill

new pjs

when your pet falls
asleep in your arms

finding a box of staples
in your drawer when
the stapler runs out

nature videos

a good coffee machine

traveler kudos from a
weathered backpack

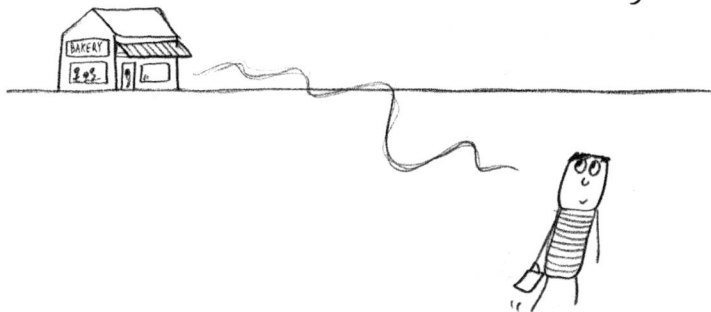

the smell of a bakery

teaching yourself
to juggle well

waking up in a new country

being deliberately
annoying

birds flying in a V

when you get called
for dinner

Dinner's
Ready!

getting the giggles

the sound of a typewriter

new art supplies

feeding a
homeless cat

a tax rebate check
in the mail

dancing in your underwear

thinking you've eaten all
your candy, but then
finding a last one down
at the bottom

a swing seat

cooking together

a sneaky nap

a generous kale salad

nature
encounters

a garden of
your own

tranquility

lids for all your tupperware

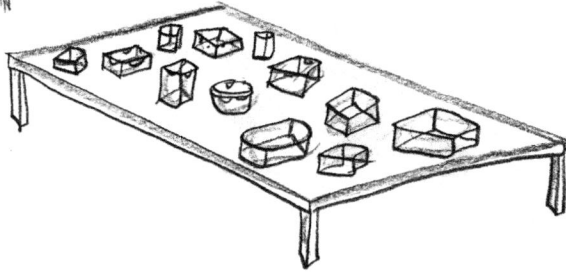

a small hotel
just when you need it

hearing a kid singing songs
your sang as a child

perfecting a difficult
guitar solo

being inspired by
where you are

a drink after work

packing a swimsuit for
a beach holiday

sitting on stairs

when the braces
come off

new pillows

laundry

traffic

tax

work

ignoring the things that annoy you

sand between your toes

a soda making machine

remembering
the whole dream from
the night before

nature's constant surprises

an afternoon of treats

MORE

being surrounded by green

as much yoga
as possible

mornings in
the park

being a caring friend

blowing a dandelion

warming your face
on a hand dryer

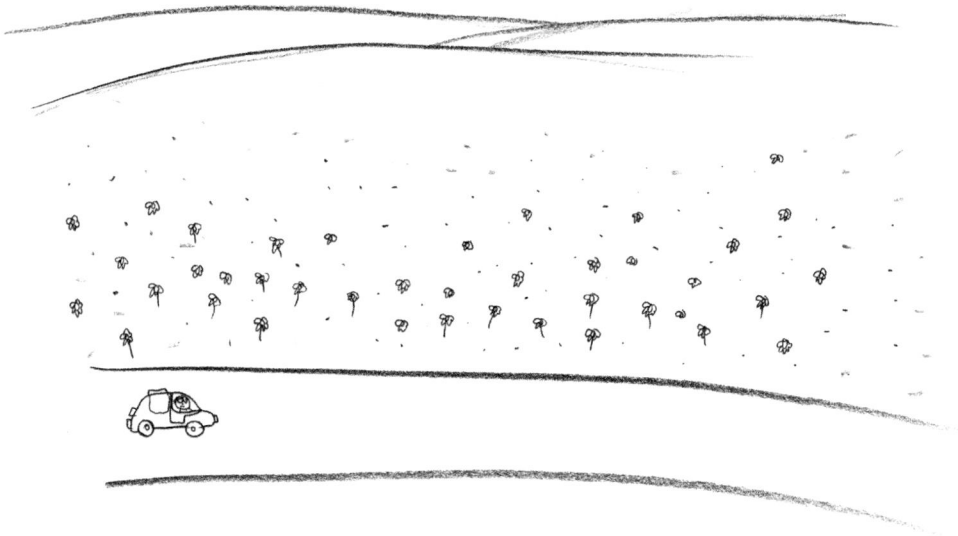

driving by fields of flowers

singing while doing
housework

when a shopkeeper
is nice to you

finding the last
hairpin when you
really need it

when someone lets you
know you have lipstick
    on your teeth
 BEFORE you head out

horsing around

knowing what you're thinking

rewatching a favorite
TV show

F.R.I.E.N.D.S

POPCORN

speeding downhill

a few free hours to
yourself

a spontaneous
back rub when
someone's putting
on sun cream

returning home

being first in line
for the buffet

the last day of school

a big hug from a small person

a lie-in

a 'woo-hoo' moment

being brought snacks when you're working hard

a really long
text exchange

putting on brand
new lipstick

a warm drink on
a chilly morning

chilling after a long
hard day

finding someone that
you feel 100%
comfortable with

seeing your favorite
band live

being surrounded by water

your luggage being
overweight for a flight
but getting away with it

cute underwear

getting obsessed with
a particular author

finding food in
the wild

discovering a jar of deli
food in the cupboard

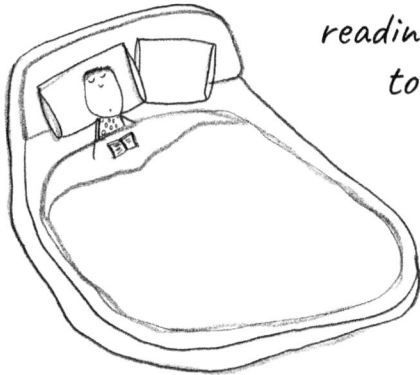

reading yourself
to sleep

putting money in
a charity box

knowing you were uncool
before uncool became
the new cool

classic family movies

making jam from the fruit of your own tree

fixing electronics by hitting them

being twirled around

the little bits of
sweet dried berries in
an otherwise boring cereal

the smell of gasoline

a drive in the countryside

seeing your mom being
amazing with your kids
and realizing she was the
same with you

wildlife photos

a basket of
freshly laid eggs

reading while
climbing the
stairs

a bicycle with a
basket

stealing back
your half of the
comforter

sharing a sense
of humor

catching a lizard

acting weird
when you're home
alone

being loved by
kids

melting chocolate
in your mouth

a straw with
a loop

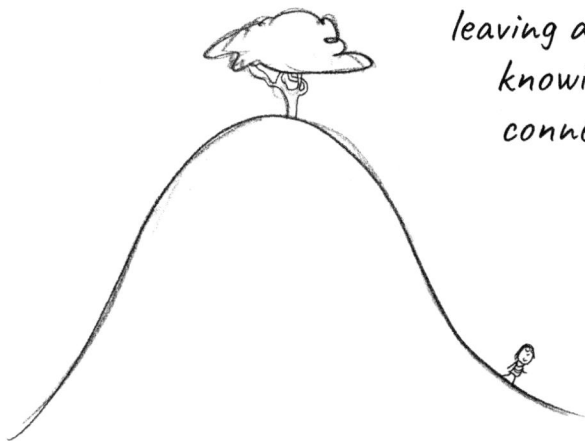

leaving a beautiful place
knowing you really
connected with it

knowing that you used the
word 'awkward' long before
it became trendy

the scent of home
after a long journey

hard-boiled eggs
on a picnic

ice-cream with
rainbow
sprinkles

organizing your bookshelf

hot chocolate
with marshmallows
on a snowy day

a meaningful
catchup

a quiet place
to work

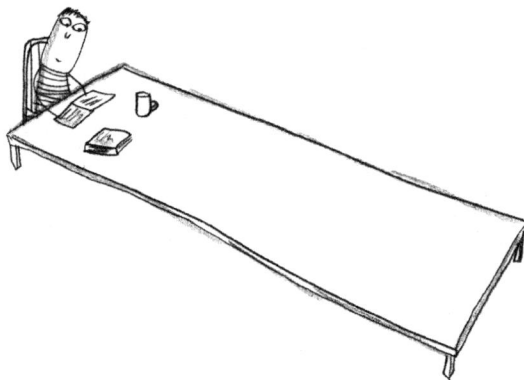

old comics

a long and much
needed pee

a deep conversation
with a child

a book that
changes your life

a ball made of
rubber bands

a totem pole

when something
glows in the dark

a great desk lamp

reorganizing
jewelry

rescuing a baby bird

realizing you're more than
halfway there

not acting
your age

your kids getting
taller than you

creating wonderful
stories in your mind
before going to sleep

a secret
smile

when the turbulence ends

Whew!

children winning
boardgames

down time

pushing a
wheelbarrow

being honest

just you and
your bike

not stepping on cracks,
no matter what

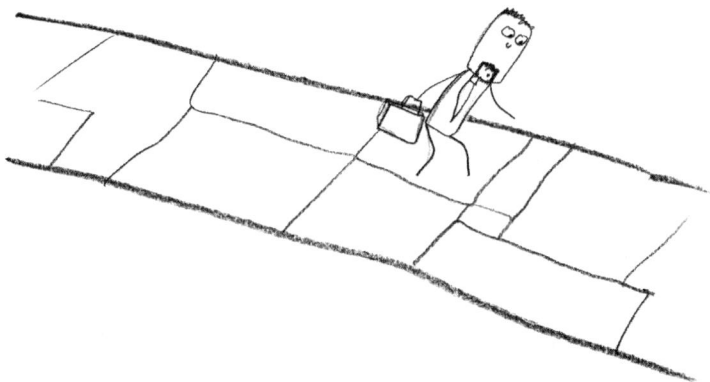

112

eating cookie dough

stretching after
waking up

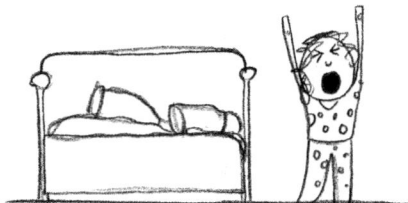

doing a silly walk

finding a lost ring

looking at photos
after a trip

waiting for
someone on the
station platform

Halfway down the stairs
is a stair, where I sit.
There isn't any other stair
quite like it...

remembering the
words of a poem you
learnt as a kid

wearing a
baby

starting your
first job

exploring a new place at dawn

the squishy faces
of sleeping children

counting your
blessings on your
fingers

when you have nail
clippers in your bag

a birthday
WEEK

skipping every
second step

more than one cupcake per person

family laughter

piling your plate at the buffet

that moment of silence
after switching off
the car engine

rereading comics from
your childhood

drinking your
favorite cocktail

being the first in line

homemade chicken soup
when you're not feeling well

getting home
early from work

catching a nice reflection of yourself

traveling solo

sliding as fast
as you can

adopting a rescue dog

a hammock that holds more than one

getting ready to jump over a wave

a cafe still open for lunch
late in the afternoon

popping
bubblewrap

helping others

curling up on a comfy
chair with a good book

meeting a friend after
years and picking up
where you left off

a giant puzzle

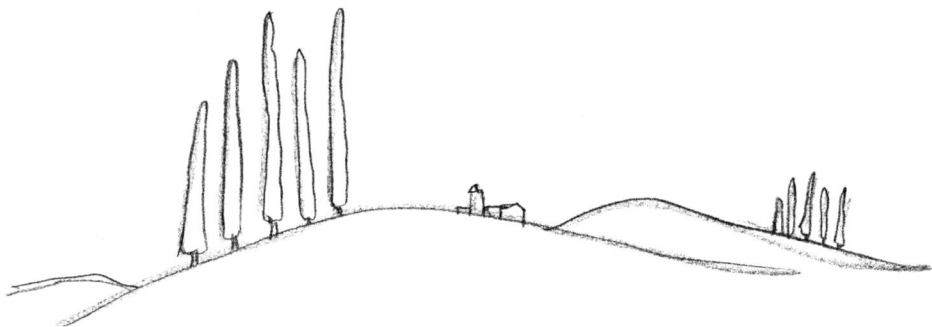

cypress trees
in the Italian countryside

a ride on the back of a pickup truck

a farm stall in the middle of nowhere

when your hair
keeps its shape

sounds and smells and light you love

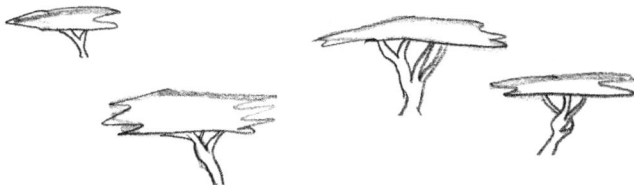

waking up a bit
sore the day after
a workout

stopping the microwave
at 1 second

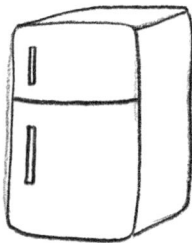

knowing there's
ice-cream in the
fridge

perfectly
smooth legs

being looked after

meeting a deadline

opening a music box

not feeling stressed
about a test

a great dance party

having the bed all
to yourself

when you juuuuust
catch the bus

whew!

cleaning ears

a handmade gift

forgiving someone you love

breathing fresh air
when you step out of
an airplane

a quiet place to work

the perfect font

a butterfly landing on skin

eating lots of cupcakes

chatting to an old friend
back home

a sweet gesture

an inside joke

creating tiny worlds

listening to the rain
when you're falling
asleep

putting long hair
into a bun when
you're sweating

a stolen nap

a baby refusing to
let go of your finger

wearing casuals
at work

finding a fresh tissue in your pocket
when you really need it

kids reading quietly in the
back of the car

adding extra hot sauce

street food

getting ready for a party

feeling brave

being called aunty
for the first time

leaving the party early

being around to help

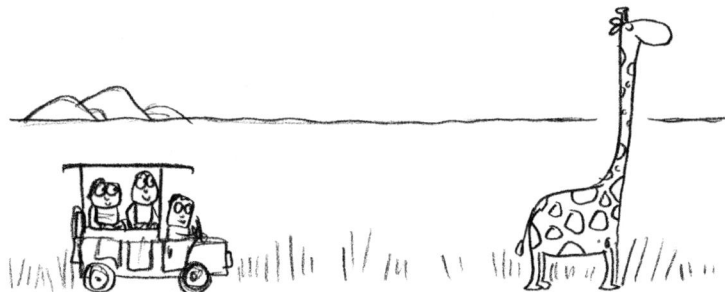

a giraffe in the wild

lazy days

when someone saves the
last chocolate for you

super-bouncy
bouncy balls

an underground fort

the first sip of a
cold drink when
you're really hot

feeling special

fun work mates

a great dance
partner

realizing that what you thought
were birds, are in fact bats

embracing
the elements

a laminating machine

being able to do that
curly thing with
your tongue

human bird calls

a neatly made bed

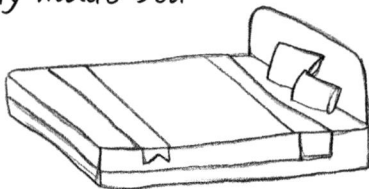

celebrating
in style

the first sip of
champagne

staring into a
fish tank

a hug that takes some of
the sadness away

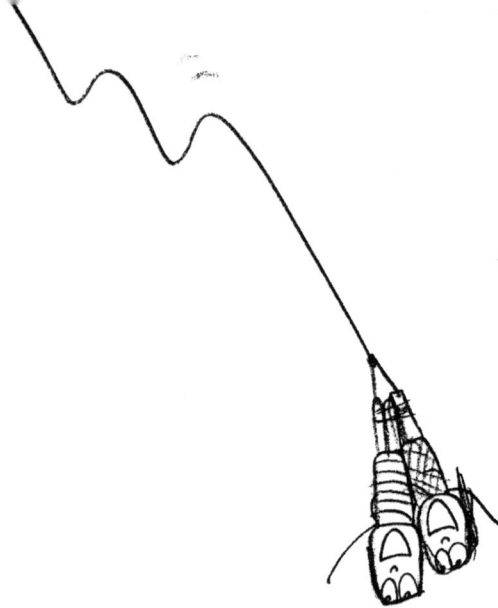

sharing the
same passions

competitive cards

a full tank of gas

sitting under a tree

wedding food

being rubbed dry with
a warm towel

a song that perfectly
describes your mood

making a baby laugh

that someone you can talk to about anything

packing a small backpack

successfully breaking into your locked car with a coat hanger

155

ice-cream straight
from the tub

DEPARTURES

heading to a destination wedding

a little boy's curls

looking through binoculars

a walk in the hills

a new razor blade

when headphones are untangled

a big bunch of balloons

dozing off during a haircut

decorating
a new home

yearly rituals

a man who sings

breakfast
in bed

a book of birds

seeing a tropical island
from a plane

when your snoring
is tolerated

getting clear directions

going off to camp

dancing like nobody's watching

a handheld
vacuum cleaner

a cold beer

accepting that everything
happens for a reason

foraging

a big family

finding money you'd
forgotten you'd hidden

the first word

when your boss goes on leave

family traditions

fresh sheets

gossiping about
a boss

ten perfectly
painted nails

staying dry under a big umbrella

dance class

when everyone says
"oooooh!" at the fireworks

a healthy ecosystem

pretending to be a
mind-reader

bed time stories

perfect meringues - outside
crunchy, inside gooey

loving nature

unlimited free
ginger at a
sushi bar

excited
children

knowing that the person
you miss is also missing you

cooking with no
recipe and no rules

a jar of pickled something, all to yourself

a warm towel when you get out of the bath in winter

uncontrollable laughter

no traffic

an ambitious project

cycling to the top
of a hill without
stopping

a flatmate who becomes
your best friend

leftover cake

getting paid

solving a hard math
problem

weirdly cool dance moves

a lap nap

turning a child's tears
into a smile

sitting down to a
perfect breakfast

friends who make the effort
to cheer you up when you're
feeling down

a vintage suitcase

a sleeping baby

french onion soup

cycling

a great hairdresser

beautiful handwriting

hilarious distractions

siesta time

dancing with eyes closed

dinner time!

Charlie Bucket winning a
Golden Ticket

eating ice-cream
straight out of the
bowl

a cool sea breeze

having a little helper

finally giving up a bad relationship

playing catch

a group of
like-minded people

holding a small
person's hand

having a cup of tea after
cleaning your home

downtime with
a newspaper

made-up stories

sea and sand between your toes

being chased by a child

close brothers

knowing you're singing the
wrong words to a song
but belting them out anyway

a whole family
on one bike

seeing fish from a pier

a perfect selfie

a light sheet on
a warm night

an over-excited dog

looking out of a plane window

"death by chocolate"

being so quiet the animals
don't run away

teaching someone who
usually teaches you

choosing ice-cream flavors

running
hand in
hand

smelling fresh coffee
grounds

giving flowers for
no reason in particular

kayaking at sunrise

having a really
good cry

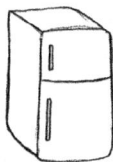

ice coming free from an ice
tray, without the usual battle

hard work that leads
to long-lasting success

being loved by
your cat

campfire ghost stories

looking fab!

waking up in a good mood

when the hiccups stop

easy, microwavable food when you're tired and just couldn't be bothered

using goggles in
the bath

a little nap at your
desk

three managing to sleep
soundly in one bed

flipping your pillow
to the cool side

buying an actual
guide book for an
upcoming trip

fertile soil

the weekend!

landing the dream job

when your rice
comes out perfectly

being the first
ones down a
snowy slope

hitting the road

when your work makes
a difference

street food

munching crunchy
food loudly to annoy
someone

a happy-ending movie
that makes you cry

a heavenly scented candle

painting easter eggs

rain when inside a tent

freshly baked bread

nuzzling

acting like weirdos

an unexpected back rub

baking the
perfect cake

the smell of a new car

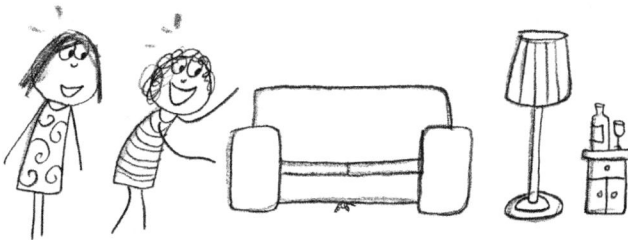

finding the missing keys

being debt free

baking for friends

flopping into bed

a crunchy juice apple

granny cuddles

a sushi date

opening a new jar
of nutella

a new album from
your favorite band

synchronized moves

ancient rock art

old perfumes reminding you of different periods of your life

rocking out

working through issues
in your diary

a very comfortable
armchair

a new handbag

securing your favorite
spot in a coffee shop

big hotel breakfasts

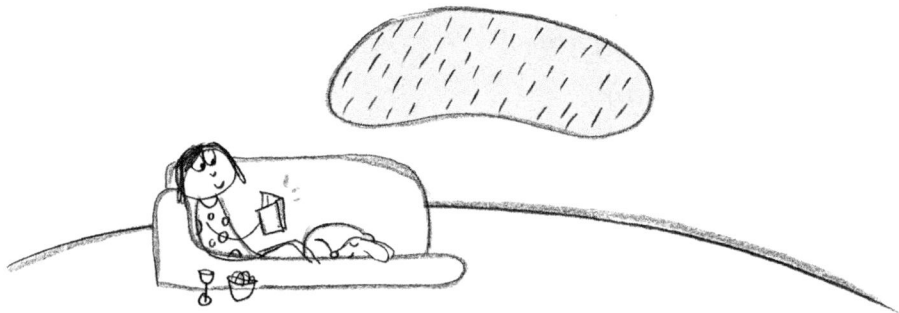

the pitter patter of rain
on the window

traveling without kids

toasting friendship

holding a helium balloon

sleeping in

instantly clicking
with someone

reading in a
bubble bath

a good selfie

a homemade birthday cake

a celebratory toast

sitting on a bench

snuggling

an unexpected upgrade

feeling like an old-fashioned
explorer

a heavy workout

total freedom

being perfectly-dressed for the weather

playing sports no matter the weather

a new perfume

a free lunch

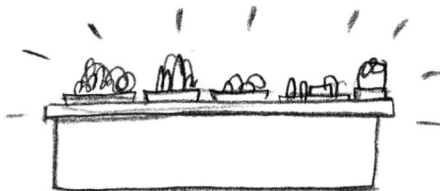

dancing like nobody's watching

a hole dug on a beach

folded laundry

learning to laugh at yourself

not growing up

old friends

buying some
happiness

CAKE

the first signs
of spring

when you stop
over-analyzing
everything

cooking to great music

squashing a mosquito

pottering around the garden

an easy day at work

rereading your
favorite book

the smell of a fresh coffee

the sound of
wind chimes

calling in sick

SALES
SHOPS
MALL

being yourself

finally getting the
pool water out of
your ear

letting go of
grudges

GRUDGE

GRUDGE

when the clouds suddenly
lift and you feel ok

taking things slower

driving with the window open and
feeling the breeze on your face

a perfect
rose

the smell of woodsmoke

a good piece of
parenting advice

realizing your kids
are growing up
to be good people

watching old
horror movies

100% phone battery

concocting a feast

watching the waves

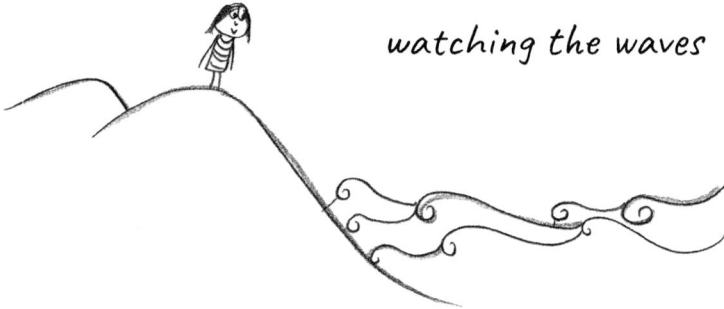

heading for
the sales

getting the last bit of
peanut butter out of
the jar

imagining you're a
famous singer

when a waiter refills the
bread basket

disco fever

living for the
moment

a giant box of
chocolates

a candlelit bath

singing your sadness away

sleepovers

a good chair
to spin on

something special in
the mail

letting go of unhelpful
thoughts

successfully
untangling
a necklace

ingredients
blending well

seeing each other
after too long apart

a glass of wine
after a long day

when you realize you are both as forgetful as each other

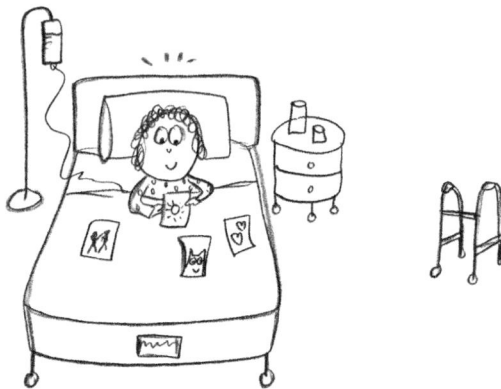

getting homemade cards when you're unwell

the smell of earth after rain

a group hug

a new dress

family in nature

hot soup on
a cold day

adopting a pet

knowing you'll
always be loved

the perfect nail
polish color

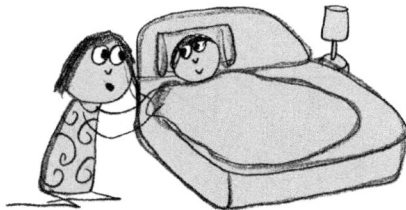

a big breakfast

appreciating the
small things

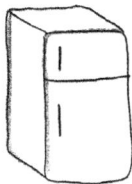

remembering you
have leftover pizza

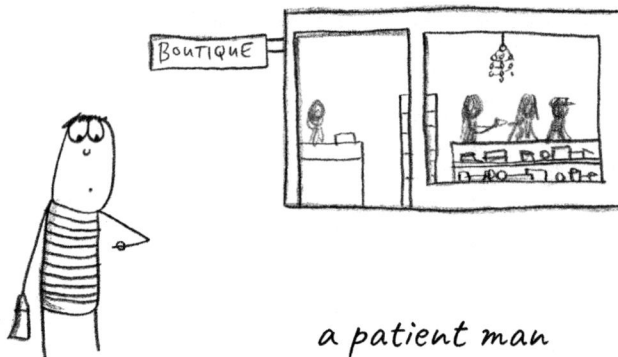

a patient man

a scintillating conversation

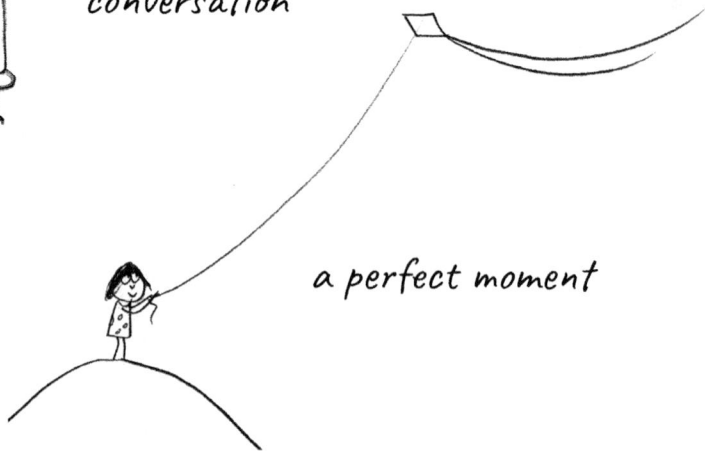

a perfect moment

230

an empty dishwasher

a good hair day

embracing your
inner couch potato

the smell of a freshly
mown lawn

an old camera
that still works

the silence of snow

a new phone

a Sunday with no plans

climbing
a tree

having a secret
language

the sea breeze

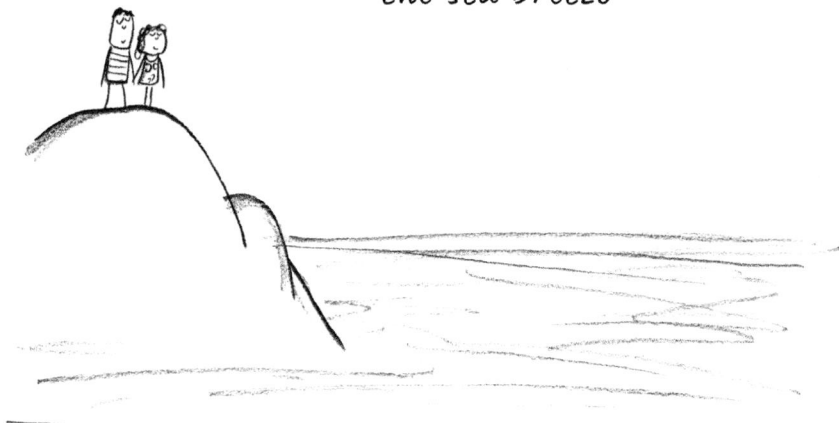

harmonies

feeling the softness
of a baby's head

getting away from the city

an extra long baguette

a bicycle made for two

toast landing with the
buttered side up

milk straight
from the
coconut

the smell of
a new book

standing up
to bullies

getting an old record player going

an intense board-game

being pampered

sun-warmed car seats

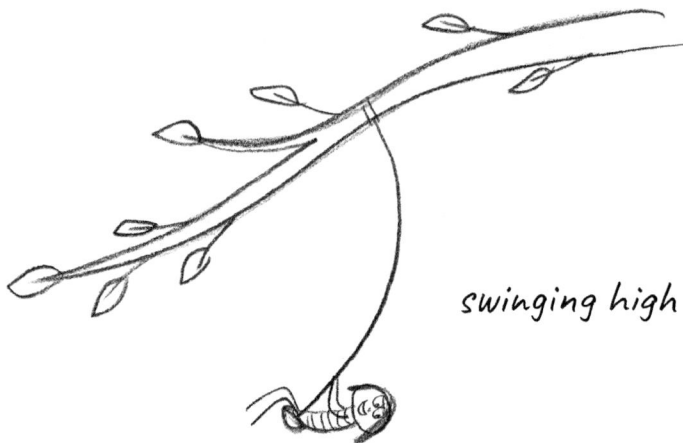

swinging high

a shared playlist

the simple things in life

pouring ice into a tub of drinks for a party you're about to have

kicking a ball around

a delicious cuddle

a bike with a basket

making
smoothies

being looked
after

water fights

a friend you're
always happy to see

dozing off

a loooong beach walk

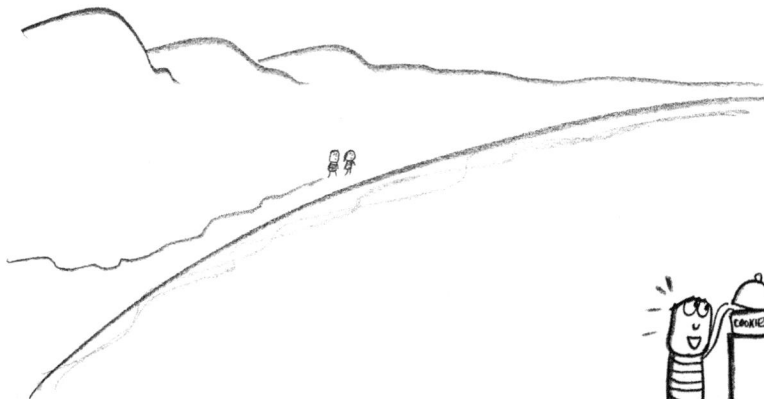

working as
a team

knowing how
you like your
tea

a secret spot

a good kisser

when the creativity
flows

pure relaxation
with no screens

a great doctor

writing a poem.

the delight of a child being
allowed to stay up late

sending photos to a
grandparent

reading the newspaper
from cover to cover

being woken
with love

having comfort
food at the end
of a stressful day

muddy puddles

a great frisbee throw

beanbags

water so clear you can see the fish

tidying up for a special visitor

exercising without watching the clock

sending a handwritten
thank you note

ice-skating

taking a
deep breath
and smiling

singing
into the wind

butterflies in your tummy for a special someone

peeling the protective sticker off a new instrument

the view from the top of a hill

a cute pet

when you both get
the urge to tidy up

blowing big
bubbles

finding a power outlet
at the airport

visiting your old neighborhood

building stuff with a pro

a back rub

making a mess

your turn on the hammock

a piggyback ride

a miniature person
suddenly appearing
in your bed

reciting a poem
by heart

'Twas brillig, and the slithy toves
  Did gyre and gimble in the wabe:
All mimsy were the borogoves,
  And the mome raths outgrabe.

sending someone flowers
for no reason

cooking on an
open fire

fabulous hair

a homemade tv

old school playground games

traveling with a friend

returning home after a long roadtrip

getting loads of small dishes

drying a little person's hair

baking with kids

hearing familiar sounds
while falling asleep

CINEMA

hanging out with
a sibling

reading to a child

a special spot

a goodnight kiss on
the forehead

family game night

being as snug as
a bug in a rug

holding your breath under
water for a long time

reorganizing
your room

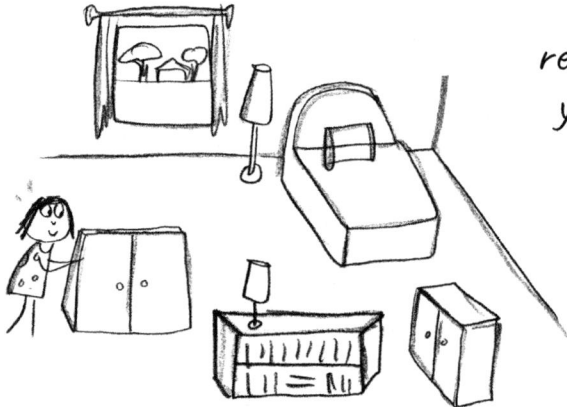

starting a journal

hanging a bird feeder

sharing freshly baked cookies

My wallet!

when your dog picks up
something you dropped
by mistake

a thoughtful
gesture

ARRIVALS

an airport reunion

unsubscribing from
random emails

finally framing those
photos

when the wind catches your kite

dropping a meal off at a
sick friend's house

playing i-spy

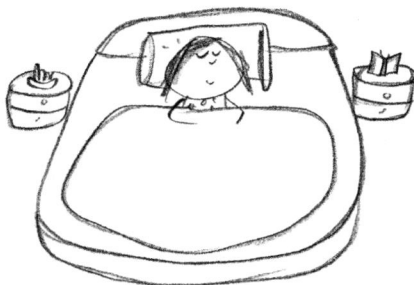

being kind to yourself

counting stars

sailing

watching calm water

running with dogs

getting the gift you've
been wanting for ages

play-chasing a baby

fairy lights

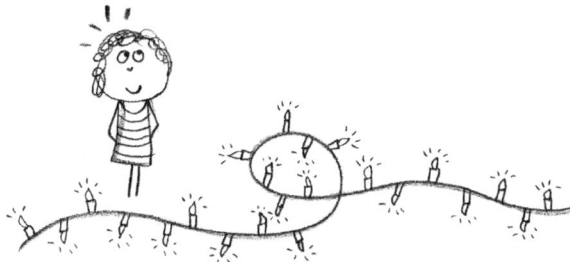

catching up

when everyone in the
family acts crazy

a waggy tail

climbing trees

SIGH

a good sigh

avoiding the microwave

sitting by an open fire

a great radio show

when you stop obsessing over
someone who's wronged you

giving money to
street performers

a clothing swap

buying a kid an ice-cream

making art

dancing like there's
no tomorrow

heading off on
an adventure

reading a classic

a desk with a view

spotting shapes
in clouds

writing a newsy
letter to
a relative

a spontaneous compliment

coffee when you *REALLY* need it

swinging a child

dressing fancy on an ordinary day

reaching the top

catching up

being encouraging

275

organizing your closet

a hearty meal

taking a long bath

complimenting a child in front of their parents

getting fresh air close to the city

treating a friend
to an outing

fixing something that's been bugging you for ages

not checking email

writing a haiku

a portrait that
captures the likeness

going the extra mile for
someone in need

a staring
competition

when you leave your phone
at home and then realize that you
feel great without it

reading in bed

letting go of the past

FUTURE

going on a
fishing trip

volunteering

RETIREMENT
VILLAGE

when the doctor gives
you a pill rather than
an injection

saying yes more often than no

hugging loved ones as often as possible

`01:06:28`

beating your personal best

cooking soup
from scratch

finding the right
Tupperware lid for
its base

cheering up someone
who's grumpy

feeling the love

making a special meal
with someone in mind

feeling the music all
through your body

helping out an elderly neighbor

being nice

being woken with a cuddle

a midday coffee run

meditating

bowls stacking
perfectly

your favorite food at the buffet

losing track of time
doing something you love

catching a fish,
whatever the size

mowing the lawn when it
really needs it

potted plants transforming a space

harvesting
vegetables

befriending an
older person

a bubble bath

inviting someone over for coffee

a great chat with a stranger when waiting in line

saying hi to people
you don't know

when the tupperware
lid goes 'click'

click

choreographing
a dance

starting a book club

laughing out loud

a little treat now and again

looking for fossils

6pm and still in pjs

enjoying the here and now instead of documenting for later

allowing others
to go first

a summer evening bike ride
for ice cream

lying in the grass
watching clouds

a community garden

going for a run without any
kind of silly gadget

coming home to
a ball of fluff

lego

stretching
your ears

finally being free after doing tons of work

realizing how good it is to be alive

having a balcony

a hosepipe with a
really strong jet

music as loud as it can be,
and singing your lungs out

bare feet on fresh grass

being satisfied
with what you have

a hot soak

maximum sleep

prioritizing friendship
and laughter

being in a good
mood

the great outdoors

being cheered on

your parents' voices when
you're far away from home

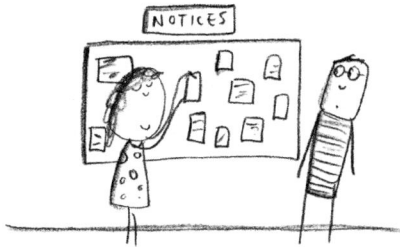

posting a notice on
an real life bulletin
board

an ambitious
sandcastle

the joy of music

filling in a family tree

sending a message in a bottle

hanging in there

donating books

being self-sufficient

a handmade card

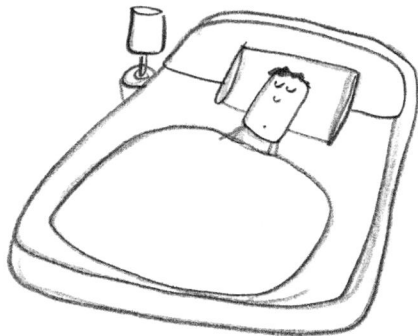
falling asleep easily

throwing fall leaves

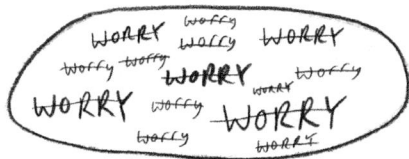

worrying less

complimenting someone's new haircut

waking up to a beautiful day

having fun

writing a list of good memories,
cutting them up and placing them
in a jar for someone as a present

a massive stretch

being impressive

making drinks for
everyone for no reason
in particular

a great jam
session

sending a sibling
a reminder of your
childhood

when a bird flies
really close to you

taking a 5 minute break outside

buying two copies of a book;
one for yourself and
another for a friend

a photo album you haven't
looked through in ages

easy chords played
really well

feeling full
of energy

a dress with
pockets

getting a plant for
your desk

cutting into delicious
cheese

putting a little money into
your savings account

drawing a portrait
of a friend

the silence before
your favorite part
of the song

finally framing
a family photo

a toothpick
working very
effectively

blowing a dandelion

five more minutes of sleep

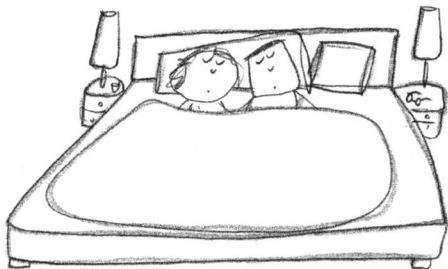

wearing something your
mother gave you, even if
you hate it

eating wild berries as you pick them

quoting a grandparent

when someone needs the safety
pin that you've been carrying
around in your bag for ages

playing a song that
reminds you of
someone special

thanking someone for
something you usually
take for granted

setting up camp

playing a game you love

having a soul sister

when the bus driver sees you running and waits

watching your
favorite movie with a
big bowl of popcorn

making a fancy
dessert

sharing memories

a spiderweb glistening
with dew

a pupil who loves
to learn

yoga first thing
in the morning

striking up a conversation with someone at the cash register

making paper snowflakes

a baby elephant

learning to trust

suddenly realizing that you don't
need to worry about the thing
that was really worrying you

working in your pjs

homemade mac
and cheese

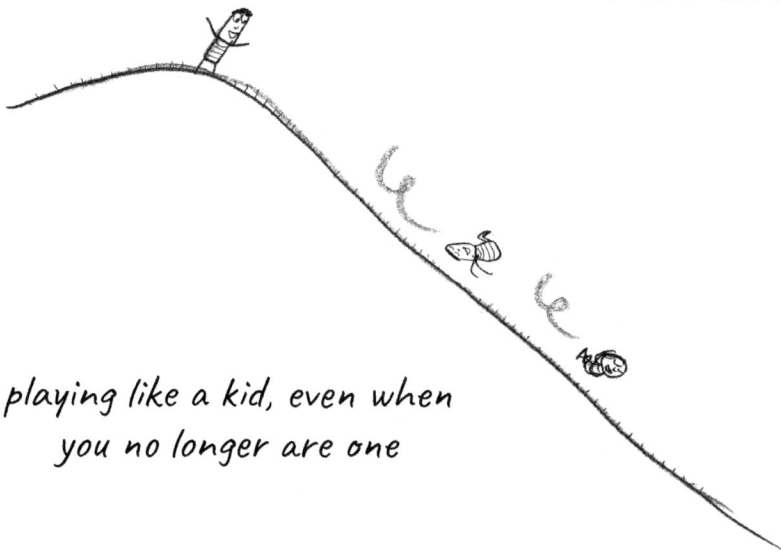

playing like a kid, even when
you no longer are one

a silent dishwasher

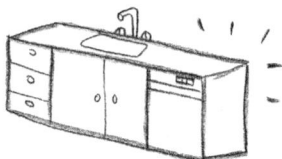

reading a children's
book in which the story
is similar to yours

using an
old-fashioned
paper map

having the freedom to
work from anywhere

She sells seashells by the seashore.
The shells she sells are surely seashells.
So if she sells shells on the seashore,
I'm sure she sells seashore shells.

a tongue twister

getting the
feeling of flying
when swimming

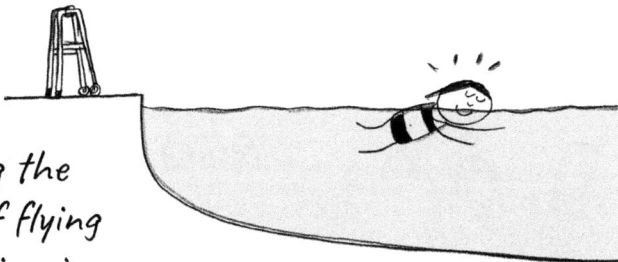

being serenaded

a tight cuddle

getting away
from it all

feeling your hands in
the soil

clearing up wires with a
neat charging station

shopping in a foreign
grocery store

the arrival of an
eagerly awaited
letter

a friend watching your children so you
can catch up with chores

getting your phone screen fixed

being looked after

support through
thick and thin

sailing on the
ocean blue

getting your
nails done

baking more than
one cake

when a new check-
out lane opens up
at the store

being on aunty duty

a singalong

a perfectly timed
hand squeeze

photos of your parent at
your age

surfing a green wave of traffic lights

predicting whether single drops of rain will run into each other as they slide down a window

a gift package

that brief delicious moment
when you're nearly asleep,
but still awake

finding the
right gym for
you

less work, more play

mom therapy

seeing your childhood
art still stuck on the
inside of your parents'
cupboard doors

FRIDAY!

a meditative activity

being immersed in the elements

tears of joy

beautiful stationery

being collected from the airport

rocking bed heads

a yoga buddy

decluttering

the first flower buds
emerging

when you're given the
heart of the artichoke

seeing a photo of yourself
on someone's fridge

organizing drawers

wearing sandals

packing away
winter clothes

sleeping in on a
drizzly day

discovering a new, sweet youtube hero you can emulate

deciding to run instead of walk

a successful partnership

the light changing
with the seasons

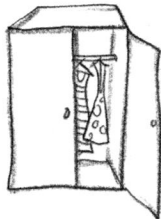

"borrowing"
clothes

buying orchids

stickers that
make you smile

a jigsaw puzzle

getting rid of stuff that you've
been hanging on to for years

being inspired by travel

telling a story in a
silly voice

when you help someone
set up their new
apartment

jumping on a bed

peace of mind

enjoying a cocktail just
before traveling

finally finishing off some
annoying admin that's been
on your mind for ages

a pile of good books

a neat room

feeling like a local

accepting change

deciding to get out of bed in ten seconds

10, 9, 8, 7, 6, 5, 4, 3, 2, 1, 1, 1, 1, 1, 1, 1, 1, 1, 1, 1, 1, 1, 1, 1, 1, 1, 1, 1, 1, 1, 1, 1, 1, 1, 1, 1, 1, 1, 1, 1, 1, 1...

unspoken sibling understanding

working out to a great playlist

going wild every
now and again

perfectly comfortable
silences

a rock song played
on a ukulele

feeling pampered

a sense of
wonder

making a duct
tape wallet

a giant
celebration

laughing at your own jokes

family breakfast and
no-one grumpy

putting the icing on

coveted shoes being on sale

hearing great news about someone you love

being inseparable

finding an information kiosk just when you need it

eating a really weird
combination of food

clean glasses

a garden of blooming sunflowers

skipping the line

VIP LANE

smiley balloons

getting an old
password right on
the first guess

playing in the shade of
a sun umbrella

when your plans are
canceled and you get
to stay in

getting home before
the storm hits

Get your own happy moment
illustrated by the artist at
www.lastlemon.com/happiness

Printed in Great Britain
by Amazon

48381741R00199